To My Girlfriend, I Want to Hear Your Story

THE GUIDED JOURNAL AND ACTIVITY BOOK FOR HER TO SHARE HER STORY WITH YOU

JEFFREY MASON

HEAR YOUR STORY BOOKS

Table of Contents

USING THIS BOOK 6
ONCE UPON A TIME 9
I WAS THIS AGE WHEN I LEARNED TO 14
LET'S CHAT ABOUT CHILDHOOD… 18
WHEN I WAS A KID, I … 24
A FEW OF MY FIRSTS 28
MY TEEN YEARS 31
WHEN I WAS A TEENAGER, I 44
MY ALL-TIME TOP 30 FAVORITE SONGS EVER PLAYLIST: 46
ADULT TIME 49
MY FIRST HOUSE/APARTMENT IN SIX QUESTIONS 52
PICK ONE 54
MY FAMILY 56
MY MOM 58
MY DAD 61
MY GRANDPARENTS 66
THE STORY OF HOW WE MET 68
THOUGHTS ON LOVE AND ROMANCE AND RELATIONSHIPS… 70
MY BOYFRIEND IN 26 LETTERS 76
SOME STUFF ABOUT ME 78
I HAVE 82
I AM GRATEFUL FOR 88
QUESTIONS ABOUT ME 92
MY TRAVEL STORIES 102
MORE QUESTIONS ABOUT ME 104
TOP 10 110
FIFTEEN THINGS I WANT 116
LOOKING FORWARD 124

This Person

_____

Gave This Person

_____

THIS BOOK BECAUSE THEY THINK (KNOW)
THEY ARE AWESOME AND WANT
TO LEARN MORE ABOUT THEM
AND THEIR LIFE STORY.

Using This Book

WOW! LOOK AT **YOU**!

YOU SHOULD PUT THOSE HANDS ON YOUR SHOULDERS, PUT YOUR HEAD BACK, AND WALK AROUND THE SCHOOL CAFETERIA LIKE YOU JUST KNOCKED REGINA GEORGE OFF HER "QUEEN BEE" THRONE.

WHY?

WELL FOR STARTERS, YOU'RE **YOU** WHICH MEANS YOU ARE BURSTING WITH ALL KINDS OF SEVERE SPECIALNESS. THERE HAS NEVER BEEN ANYONE LIKE YOU AND THERE WILL NEVER BE ANYONE LIKE YOU AGAIN (WE'RE SAYING THAT IN A NICE WAY.)

ANOTHER REASON? WELL, IF YOU HAVE THIS BOOK, IT IS BECAUSE YOU HAVE A **SOMEONE SPECIAL** YOU ARE GIVING IT TO...

OR...

SOMEONE SPECIAL GAVE IT TO **YOU** BECAUSE THEY WANT TO LEARN A WHOLE BUNCH MORE ABOUT **YOU**.

IF YOU ASK US, BOTH ARE PRETTY AWESOME.

WE TOLD **YOU** THAT YOU ARE PRETTY DANG SPECIAL AND SPECTACULAR.

SO, WHAT'S THE DEAL WITH THIS BOOK?

THE DEAL IS THAT THIS BOOK WAS MADE SO YOU COULD HAVE ALL KINDS OF **FUN** SHARING THE TALE AND TALES OF **YOU**.

EACH PAGE IS PLUM FULL OF QUESTIONS AND ACTIVITIES, EXPERTLY DESIGNED TO GUIDE **YOU** IN SHARING A LITTLE (OR MORE) OF **YOUR** LIFE STORY.

THERE ARE QUESTIONS ABOUT YOUR CHILDHOOD AND TEENS AND FAMILY AND DREAMS AND GOALS. THERE ARE OTHERS THAT GIVE YOU ROOM TO SAY, "HERE IS WHAT I THINK."

THERE ARE ALSO A FEW (JUST A FEW) THAT ARE A LITTLE DEEP AND REQUIRE A BIT OF VULNERABILITY (BUT IN A GOOD WAY).

THAT SAID, **YOU** GET TO DECIDE HOW MUCH **YOU** WANT TO SHARE.

LASTLY, THERE ARE OPPORTUNITIES TO TALK ABOUT THAT **SOMEONE SPECIAL**. THIS BOOK GIVES YOU ROOM TO SHARE WHAT YOU THINK ABOUT THEM, YOUR MEMORIES, AND EVEN WHAT YOUR BEST GUESS IS ON WHAT **THEY** WOULD SAY.

SO, GET OUT A PENCIL OR A PEN AND A BEVERAGE OF YOUR CHOICE, AND LET YOURSELF SHARE A BUNCH ABOUT **YOU**.

THEN PASS IT BACK TO THE PERSON WHO GAVE IT TO **YOU** AND SEE WHAT WOWS THEM. AND THEN TALK. TALKING IS GREAT!

AND HAVE **FUN**. DEFINITELY THAT!

"He stepped down, trying not to look long at her, as if she were the sun, yet he saw her, like the sun, even without looking."
- "Anna Karenina" by Leo Tolstoy

Once Upon a Time

(THAT MEANS "IN THE PAST" IN FAIRY TALE PRINCESS LANGUAGE)

SHARE A LITTLE ABOUT THE DAY YOU WERE BORN:

THIS IS THE DAY I WAS BORN

_____

I WAS BORN IN THIS TOWN...

_____

AND THE PLACE I WAS BORN WAS (HOSPITAL, AT HOME, SIDE OF THE ROAD, ETC.) ...

_____

_____

MY FULL NAME AT BIRTH WAS...

_____

_____

THIS NAME WAS SELECTED FOR ME BECAUSE...

_____

_____

_____

_____

IF THEY HAD ASKED ME, I WOULD HAVE ASKED TO BE NAMED…

_____

_____

THIS IS HOW MUCH I WEIGHED WHEN I WAS BORN…

_____

AND I WAS THIS LONG…

_____

WHEN I WAS BORN, MY PARENT'S AGES WERE…

_____

_____

MY FIRST WORDS WERE…

_____

_____

_____

AND I TOOK MY FIRST STEPS AT THIS AGE…

_____

_____

(If you were adopted...)

I WAS THIS AGE WHEN MY PARENTS ADOPTED ME...

_____

AND I WAS THIS AGE WHEN I FOUND OUT I HAD BEEN ADOPTED...

_____

I WAS TOLD BY...

_____

I WOULD DESCRIBE MYSELF WHEN I WAS A KID THIS WAY...

_____

_____

_____

_____

THIS IS WHAT I KNOW ABOUT MY BIRTH PARENTS...

_____

_____

_____

_____

WHEN MY PARENTS AND OTHERS TALK ABOUT HOW I WAS AS A BABY, THEY DESCRIBE ME THIS WAY (ANSWER WITH A DESCRIPTION, POEM, OR DRAWING.) ...

"I'm looking into your eyes because I want to see what you see."
- Abigail Jeffries

I was this age when I learned to...

- SAY MY A, B, C'S: _____
- READ: _____
- WRITE MY NAME: _____
- WRITE MY NAME IN CURSIVE: _____
- GET DRESSED BY MYSELF: _____
- TIE MY SHOES: _____
- TIE A TIE: _____
- SHAVE: _____
- DO LAUNDRY: _____
- IRON: _____
- VACUUM: _____
- SEW ON A BUTTON: _____
- USE A SCREWDRIVER: _____
- USE A SAW: _____
- CHANGE A LIGHTBULB: _____
- UNCLOG A TOILET: _____
- PAINT A WALL: _____
- DO A CARTWHEEL: _____
- ROLLER SKATE: _____
- SKATEBOARD: _____

I was this age when I learned to...

- RIDE A BIKE (TWO-WHEEL): _____
- RIDE A HORSE: _____
- RIDE A MOTORCYCLE: _____
- DRIVE A CAR: _____
- PARALLEL PARK: _____
- DRIVE A STICK SHIFT CAR: _____
- CHANGE A TIRE: _____
- CHANGE THE OIL IN A CAR: _____
- SWIM: _____
- DIVE FROM A DIVING BOARD: _____
- WATER SKI: _____
- SURF: _____
- SCUBA DIVE: _____
- RIDE A SLED: _____
- SNOW SKI: _____
- SNOW BOARD: _____
- CATCH A BALL: _____
- THROW A BALL: _____
- SLOW DANCE: _____
- FAST DANCE: _____

I was this age when I learned to...

- WHISTLE: _____
- PLAY A MUSICAL INSTRUMENT: _____
- SHAKE HANDS: _____
- PROPERLY KISS: _____
- PLAY SPIN THE BOTTLE: _____
- APPRECIATE WHAT "THE BIRDS AND THE BEES" REALLY MEANS: _____
- MAKE A CUP OF COFFEE: _____
- OPEN A BOTTLE OF WINE (CORKED): _____
- MAKE A COCKTAIL: _____
- GROCERY SHOP: _____
- COOK A MEAL FOR A GROUP OF PEOPLE: _____
- SET THE TABLE: _____
- DO DISHES: _____
- DO ADDITION AND SUBTRACTION: _____
- DO MULTIPLICATION AND DIVISION: _____
- TELL TIME: _____
- WRITE A CHECK: _____
- DO MY TAXES: _____
- MAKE A RESUME: _____

I was this age when I learned to...

- INTERVIEW FOR A JOB: _____
- VOTE: _____
- MAKE MY OWN DOCTOR/DENTIST APPOINTMENT: _____
- READ A MAP: _____
- HOLD A BABY: _____
- CHANGE A DIAPER: _____
- CALM A CRYING BABY: _____
- FEED A BABY: _____
- SHUFFLE CARDS: _____
- DO A CARD TRICK: _____
- PLAY POKER: _____
- PLAY BLACKJACK: _____
- PLAY POOL: _____
- FISH: _____
- SHOOT A GUN: _____
- CHOP WOOD: _____
- SET UP A TENT: _____
- START A CAMPFIRE: _____
- THROW A PUNCH: _____
- BLOCK A PUNCH: _____

Let's chat about childhood...

WHEN I WAS A KID, MOST PEOPLE CALLED ME...

_____

BUT SOMETIMES THEY WOULD USE THIS NICKNAME...

_____

I WAS GIVEN THIS NICKNAME BECAUSE...

_____

_____

I WOULD DESCRIBE MYSELF WHEN I WAS A KID THIS WAY...

_____

_____

_____

...AND MY CHILDHOOD THIS WAY...

_____

_____

_____

DURING MY ELEMENTARY SCHOOL YEARS, MY BEST FRIENDS WERE...

_____

_____

_____

_____

THE LAST TIME I SPOKE WITH ANY OF THEM WAS...

_____

_____

_____

_____

THE ELEMENTARY SCHOOL TEACHER THAT I MOST FONDLY REMEMBER IS...

_____

THE THING I MOST REMEMBER ABOUT THIS TEACHER IS...

_____

_____

_____

WHEN I WAS A KID, MY REGULAR CHORES INCLUDED...

_____

_____

_____

_____

IN RETURN, I RECEIVED AN ALLOWANCE OF...

_____

_____

WHEN I HAD MONEY, I WOULD TYPICALLY SPEND IT ON...

_____

_____

_____

_____

WHEN I WAS A KID, I DREAMED OF BECOMING A...

_____

_____

_____

_____

ONE OF MY MOST FAVORITE CHILDHOOD MEMORIES IS...

DURING MY CHILDHOOD, I SPENT MOST OF MY SUMMERS DOING THIS...

_____

_____

_____

_____

THIS IS WHERE WE LIVED DURING MY ELEMENTARY AND JUNIOR HIGH SCHOOL YEARS...

_____

_____

_____

THIS IS HOW I WOULD DESCRIBE WHERE WE LIVED...

_____

_____

_____

_____

_____

_____

IF I COULD BE A KID AGAIN FOR JUST ONE DAY, I WOULD DO FOLLOWING (ANSWER WITH A DESCRIPTION, POEM, OR DRAWING.)
...

When I was a kid, I ...

- ☐ HAD AN IMAGINARY FRIEND.
- ☐ SHARED A BEDROOM.
- ☐ HAD TO SLEEP WITH A SPECIFIC TOY OR BLANKET.
- ☐ HAD A NIGHT LIGHT.
- ☐ LIKED TO BE TUCKED IN.
- ☐ WAS READ BEDTIME STORIES.
- ☐ WALKED TO SCHOOL.
- ☐ RODE MY BIKE TO SCHOOL.
- ☐ GOT A DETENTION.
- ☐ WAS SENT TO THE PRINCIPAL'S OFFICE.
- ☐ WAS IN A SCHOOL PLAY.
- ☐ HAD A CRUSH ON A CLASSMATE.
- ☐ HAD A CRUSH ON SOMEONE FAMOUS.
- ☐ WAS IN A SCHOOL SPELLING BEE.
- ☐ CAMPED IN THE BACKYARD.
- ☐ MADE FORTS.
- ☐ HAD A TREEHOUSE.
- ☐ CAUGHT FIREFLIES.
- ☐ HAD A TELESCOPE.
- ☐ WENT TO SUMMER CAMP.
- ☐ COLLECTED SHELLS ON THE BEACH.
- ☐ MADE A SANDCASTLE.

When I was a kid, I ...

- ☐ HAD A REPTILE, INSECT, OR ARACHNID FOR A PET.
- ☐ WAS IN A SNOWBALL FIGHT.
- ☐ MADE A SNOWMAN.
- ☐ HAD A LEMONADE STAND.
- ☐ HAD A PAPER ROUTE.
- ☐ TOOK MUSIC LESSONS.
- ☐ FLEW A KITE.
- ☐ ROLLER-SKATED.
- ☐ RODE A SKATEBOARD.
- ☐ READ COMIC BOOKS.
- ☐ COLLECTED SPORTS CARDS.
- ☐ PLAYED SPORTS.
- ☐ TOOK MARTIAL ARTS.
- ☐ GOT MONEY FROM THE TOOTH FAIRY.
- ☐ GOT ICE CREAM FROM AN ICE CREAM TRUCK.
- ☐ HAD SLEEPOVERS.
- ☐ SNUCK OUT OF THE HOUSE AT NIGHT.
- ☐ WROTE ON THE WALLS.
- ☐ WENT TO THE ZOO.
- ☐ WENT TO AN AMUSEMENT PARK.
- ☐ BROKE A BONE.
- ☐ HAD TO GET STICHES.

When I was a kid, I ...

I REMEMBER PLAYING THESE GAMES...

___

AND WITH THESE TOYS...

___

AND LOVING THESE TELEVISION SHOWS...

___

When I was a kid, I ...

AND THESE MOVIES...

_____

AND THESE SONGS...

_____

AND THESE BOOKS...

A few of my firsts...

MY FIRST PET WAS A...

___

ITS NAME WAS...

___

I GOT MY FIRST CAR WHEN I WAS THIS AGE...

___

THE FIRST CAR I OWNED ON MY OWN WAS A (YEAR, MAKE, AND MODEL)...

___

I GOT MY FIRST TRAFFIC TICKET WHEN I WAS THIS AGE...

___

I RECEIVED THIS TICKET BECAUSE...

___

___

___

AND THIS IS WHAT I HAD TO DO AND PAY...

___

___

___

THE FIRST ALBUM/TAPE/CD I CAN REMEMBER BUYING WAS...

THE FIRST MUSIC CONCERT I ATTENDED WAS...

MY FIRST IMPRESSIONS OF MY BOYFRIEND WERE...

"I've tried so many times to think of a new way to say it, and it's still I love you." – Zelda Fitzgerald

My teen years...

I WOULD DESCRIBE MYSELF WHEN I WAS A TEENAGER THIS WAY...

THIS IS HOW I DRESSED AND STYLED MY HAIR DURING MY HIGH SCHOOL YEARS...

_____

_____

_____

_____

_____

_____

_____

_____

_____

_____

_____

_____

PASTE A PICTURE OF YOU FROM YOUR HIGH SCHOOL YEARS.

DURING MY TEENAGE YEARS, THE PEOPLE I MAINLY HUNG OUT WITH WERE...

_____

_____

_____

_____

_____

THE LAST TIME WE TALKED WAS...

_____

_____

_____

MY PARENTS' OPINION OF MY CHOICE IN FRIENDS WAS...

_____

_____

_____

_____

A TYPICAL WEEKEND NIGHT DURING MY HIGH SCHOOL YEARS WAS SPENT...

___

___

___

___

___

MY CURFEW IN HIGH SCHOOL WAS...

___

___

ONE MEMORABLE TIME I MISSED MY CURFEW WAS BECAUSE...

___

___

___

___

___

MY PARENTS' REACTION TO MY MISSING CURFEW WAS...

_____

_____

_____

_____

_____

THE THREE WORDS I WOULD USE TO DESCRIBE MY HIGH SCHOOL DATING LIFE ARE...

_____

_____

_____

I GOT MY DRIVER'S LICENSE WHEN I WAS THIS AGE...

_____

TO GET MY LICENSE, I HAD TO TAKE MY DRIVING TEST THIS MANY TIMES...

_____

THE PERSON WHO TAUGHT ME TO DRIVE WAS...

_____

_____

THE YEAR, MAKE, AND MODEL OF THE CAR I LEARNED HOW TO DRIVE IN WAS...

_____

_____

THE YEAR I GRADUATED I FROM HIGH SCHOOL WAS...

_____

MY GRADUATING CLASS HAD THIS MANY STUDENTS IN IT...

_____

MY GRADES WERE TYPICALLY IN THIS RANGE...

_____

_____

_____

MY FAVORITE AND LEAST FAVORITE SUBJECTS WERE...

_____

_____

_____

_____

THE THINGS I LIKED THE MOST ABOUT HIGH SCHOOL WERE...

_____

_____

_____

_____

_____

_____

_____

...AND THESE ARE THE THINGS I COULD HAVE DONE WITHOUT...

_____

_____

_____

_____

_____

_____

_____

THE SCHOOL ACTIVITIES AND SPORTS THAT I PARTICIPATED IN WERE...

WHEN I WAS A TEENAGER, I SPENT MY SUMMERS...

KNOWING WHAT I KNOW NOW, THE ADVICE I WOULD GIVE MY TEENAGE SELF IS...

_____

_____

_____

_____

_____

_____

_____

_____

_____

_____

_____

_____

_____

A TEACHER, COACH, OR MENTOR THAT HAD A HUGE IMPACT ON ME BECOMING WHO I AM TODAY IS...

_____

_____

_____

THE SPECIFIC INFLUENCES THEY HAD ON ME, AND MY LIFE WERE...

_____

_____

_____

_____

_____

_____

_____

_____

MY BEDROOM FROM MY TEENAGE YEARS LOOKED LIKE THIS...

IF I HAD TO DESCRIBE IT, I WOULD SAY THE OVERALL THEME WAS...

_____

_____

_____

THE WALLS WERE THIS COLOR...

_____

_____

MY BEDDING LOOKED LIKE THIS...

_____

_____

I HAD THESE THINGS ON THE WALLS...

_____

_____

_____

_____

_____

AND MY FAVORITE PLACE TO HIDE THINGS WAS...

ADDITIONAL IMPORTANT DETAILS INCLUDE...

When I was a teenager, I...

LOVED THESE BANDS/MUSICIANS...

AND THESE BOOKS...

When I was a teenager...

AND THESE MOVIES...

___

AND THESE TELEVISION SHOWS...

My all-time Top 30 favorite songs ever playlist:

1. _____
2. _____
3. _____
4. _____
5. _____
6. _____
7. _____
8. _____
9. _____
10. _____
11. _____
12. _____
13. _____
14. _____
15. _____

16. ___
17. ___
18. ___
19. ___
20. ___
21. ___
22. ___
23. ___
24. ___
25. ___
26. ___
27. ___
28. ___
29. ___
30. ___

"The best thing to hold onto in life is each other." - Audrey Hepburn

Adult time...

AFTER HIGH SCHOOL I MADE THE CHOICE TO...

- ☐ START COLLEGE.
- ☐ JOIN THE MILITARY.
- ☐ GET A JOB.
- ☐ TAKE A BREAK.
- ☐ OTHER: _____

I MADE THIS DECISION BECAUSE...

_____
_____
_____
_____
_____
_____
_____

LOOKING BACK, THIS IS HOW I NOW FEEL ABOUT MY DECISION...

- ☐ IT WAS THE RIGHT ONE, AT THE RIGHT TIME.
- ☐ IT WAS THE RIGHT DIRECTION TO GO IN, BUT THE WRONG TIME TO DO IT.
- ☐ YOU CAN'T GET THEM ALL RIGHT.
- ☐ THE JURY'S STILL OUT.

I THINK THAT THIS WAS THE CORRECT OR INCORRECT DECISION BECAUSE...

_____
_____
_____
_____
_____
_____

THIS IS HOW THIS PERIOD IMPACTED MY LIFE...

_____
_____
_____
_____
_____
_____
_____

IF I HAD A REDO, I WOULD MAKE THESE CHANGES TO THIS PERIOD OF MY LIFE...

_____

_____

_____

_____

_____

_____

_____

I GOT MY FIRST JOB WHEN I WAS THIS AGE...

_____

THE JOB WAS...

_____

_____

_____

...AND I WAS PAID THIS MUCH...

_____

My first house/apartment in six questions...

THE FIRST PLACE I LIVED ON MY OWN OR WITH ROOMMATES WAS...

_____

_____

I MOVED HERE WHEN I WAS THIS AGE...

_____

IT HAD THIS MANY BEDROOMS AND BATHROOMS...

_____

_____

I LIVED THERE WITH...

_____

_____

_____

_____

MY SHARE OF THE RENT/MORTGAGE WAS...

_____

_____

My first apartment in six questions...

THIS IS HOW I WOULD DESCRIBE THIS PLACE...

Pick One...
(EXTRA CREDIT IF YOUR MARK WHAT YOU THINK YOUR BOYFRIEND WOULD SELECT)

CARD GAMES	OR	BOARD GAMES
STREAMING	OR	VINYL
NICE HOUSE	OR	NICE CAR
BEACH	OR	WOODS
SETTLE DOWN SOON	OR	SETTLE DOWN EVENTUALLY
BEER OR WINE	OR	COCKTAILS
CALL	OR	TEXT
CHANGE THE PAST	OR	SEE THE FUTURE
BOOK VERSION	OR	MOVIE VERSION
WEEKLY RELIGIOUS SERVICES	OR	I HAVE MY OWN BELIEFS
LIVE IN TOWN	OR	LIVE ON LOTS OF LAND
TENT	OR	CABIN
PANCAKES	OR	WAFFLES
WORK OVERTIME	OR	FREE TIME
CHURCH WEDDING	OR	OUTDOOR WEDDING
I PREFER TO DRIVE	OR	I'M GOOD IF HE DRIVES
PLAY VIDEO GAMES	OR	WATCH TELEVISION
LIGHT PACKER	OR	HEAVY PACKER
RELAXING VACATION	OR	EXPLORING VACATION

Pick One...

CARDIO	OR	LIFTING WEIGHTS
MOVIE AT THE THEATER	OR	MOVIE AT HOME
BOOK	OR	EBOOK
I STRICTLY FOLLOW A BUDGET	OR	I KNOW WHAT I CAN SPEND
HAVE KIDS ONE DAY	OR	NOT SURE/NOT FOR ME
SALTY	OR	SWEET
CAR	OR	TRUCK
SPEND	OR	SAVE/INVEST
COOK AT HOME	OR	ORDER IN/EAT OUT
DOUBLE INCOME	OR	STAY-AT-HOME PARENT
SMALL TOWN	OR	BIG CITY
WEEKENDS HOME	OR	WEEKENDS OUT
THINK FIRST	OR	LEAP FIRST
OPEN-MINDED	OR	KNOW WHAT I BELIEVE
ME: A LITTLE DEBT	OR	ME: A LOT OF DEBT
MAKE IT WORK	OR	TRY SOMETHING ELSE
OUTSIDE	OR	INDOORS
EXERCISE OFTEN	OR	EXERCISE SOMETIMES
WANT PETS	OR	NO PETS

My family...

THE THREE WORDS I WOULD USE TO DESCRIBE MY FAMILY ARE...

1. _____

2. _____

3. _____

THE TELEVISION FAMILY THAT REMINDS ME THE MOST OF MY FAMILY WHEN I WAS GROWING UP IS...

_____

_____

I HAVE THIS MANY BROTHERS AND SISTERS...

_____

I WAS THE OLDEST/MIDDLE/YOUNGEST OR ONLY CHILD...

_____

IN ORDER OF THEIR BIRTH, MY SIBLINGS' NAMES ARE...

_____

_____

_____

_____

My family...

A REALLY COOL FUN FACT ABOUT MY FAMILY IS...

THE HOLIDAY THAT WAS THE BIGGEST DEAL IN OUR FAMILY WAS...

A FEW OF THE WAYS WE CELEBRATED THIS HOLIDAY INCLUDED...

My mom...

MY MOTHER'S FULL NAME IS...
_____

THE WAY I WOULD DESCRIBE HER IS...
_____
_____
_____
_____
_____
_____
_____
_____
_____

THIS IS WHERE SHE WAS BORN AND GREW UP...
_____
_____
_____

A REALLY COOL FUN FACT ABOUT MY MOTHER IS...

_____

_____

_____

_____

HER HIGHEST LEVEL OF EDUCATION AND OCCUPATIONS ARE...

_____

_____

_____

SHE AND I ARE ALIKE IN THESE WAYS...

_____

_____

_____

_____

_____

_____

ONE OF MY FAVORITE MEMORIES OF MY MOTHER IS...

_____

_____

_____

_____

_____

_____

_____

SOME OF THE BEST ADVICE SHE EVER GAVE ME WAS...

_____

_____

_____

_____

_____

_____

My dad...

MY FATHER'S FULL NAME IS...

___

THE WAY I WOULD DESCRIBE HIM IS...

___

___

___

___

___

___

___

___

THIS IS WHERE HE WAS BORN AND GREW UP...

___

___

___

A REALLY COOL FUN FACT ABOUT MY FATHER IS...

HIS HIGHEST LEVEL OF EDUCATION AND OCCUPATIONS IS...

HE AND I ARE ALIKE IN THESE WAYS...

ONE OF MY FAVORITE MEMORIES OF MY FATHER IS...

_____

_____

_____

_____

_____

_____

_____

_____

SOME OF THE BEST ADVICE HE EVER GAVE ME WAS...

_____

_____

_____

_____

_____

_____

_____

MY PARENTS WERE MARRIED WHEN THEY WERE THIS AGE...

_____

_____

THEY HAVE BEEN/WERE MARRIED FOR THIS MANY YEARS...

_____

I WOULD DESCRIBE THEIR RELATIONSHIP THIS WAY...

_____

_____

_____

_____

THEIR RELATIONSHIP INFLUENCED HOW I FEEL ABOUT LOVE, RELATIONSHIPS, AND MARRIAGE IN THE FOLLOWING WAYS...

_____

_____

_____

_____

_____

I WOULD DESCRIBE MY RELATIONSHIP WITH MY PARENTS WHEN I WAS A KID THIS WAY...

_____

_____

_____

_____

...AND THIS WAY DURING MY TEENS...

_____

_____

_____

_____

...AND NOW...

_____

_____

_____

_____

My grandparents...

MY GRANDPARENTS' NAMES ON MY MOTHER'S SIDE ARE...

_____

MY GRANDPARENTS' NAMES ON MY FATHER'S SIDE ARE...

_____

THIS IS WHAT I CALLED THEM...

_____

_____

THIS IS HOW I WOULD DESCRIBE MY MOTHER'S PARENTS...

_____

_____

_____

THIS IS HOW I WOULD DESCRIBE MY FATHER'S PARENTS...

_____

_____

_____

A LIST OF PEOPLE OTHER THAN MY PARENTS WHO HELPED RAISE ME INCLUDES...

1. _____
2. _____
3. _____
4. _____
5. _____
6. _____
7. _____
8. _____
9. _____
10. _____
11. _____
12. _____
13. _____
14. _____
15. _____

The Story of How We Met...

USE THESE TWO PAGES TO TELL THE STORY OF HOW AND YOU YOUR BOYFRIEND MET AS THOUGH IT WAS A FAIRY TALE.

FEEL FREE TO INCLUDE DRAGONS TO BE SLAIN, FROGS TO BE KISSED, SPELLS TO BE BROKEN, KNIGHTS IN SHINING ARMOR, AND PRINCESSES IN DISTRESS.

Once upon a time ago, in a land far, far away

_____

_____

_____

_____

_____

_____

_____

_____

_____

Thoughts on love and romance and relationships...

IN MY OPINION, THE FIVE MOST IMPORTANT FACTORS IN KEEPING A RELATIONSHIP STRONG AND HEALTHY ARE...

1. _____
2. _____
3. _____
4. _____
5. _____

THE COUPLE I THINK IS A MODEL FOR A GREAT RELATIONSHIP IS...

_____
_____

THE QUALITIES I MOST ADMIRE ABOUT THEIR RELATIONSHIP ARE...

_____
_____
_____
_____
_____

I CAN TELL I AM DEVELOPING FEELINGS FOR SOMEONE WHEN I START TO...

_____

_____

_____

_____

MY TOP THREE RELATIONSHIP DEAL BREAKERS ARE...

1. _____

2. _____

3. _____

IF I WERE PLANNING MY VERSION OF THE PERFECT DATE NIGHT, IT WOULD INCLUDE ALL THE FOLLOWING...

_____

_____

_____

_____

_____

_____

THE DESTINATION I WOULD PICK AS THE PERFECT ROMANTIC VACATION IS...

_____

_____

_____

MY FAVORITE ROMANTIC MOVIE IS...

_____

_____

AND THIS IS MY FAVORITE ROMANTIC SONG...

_____

_____

I WAS THIS AGE WHEN...

    I HAD MY FIRST CRUSH: _____

    I WENT ON MY FIRST DATE: _____

    I HAD MY FIRST KISS: _____

    I WAS IN MY FIRST STEADY RELATIONSHIP: _____

    MY HEART WAS BROKEN THE FIRST TIME: _____

    MET MY GIRLFRIEND: _____

ACCORDING TO THE BOOK, "THE 5 LOVE LANGUAGES," EACH OF US HAS A SPECIFIC WAY WE EXPRESS AND FEEL LOVE. THE FIVE WAYS ARE: WITH WORDS THAT SHOW AFFECTION, PRAISE AND APPRECIATION; SPENDING FOCUSED TIME TOGETHER; PHYSICAL AND AFFECTIONATE TOUCH; DOING NICE THINGS FOR EACH OTHER; GIVING AND RECEIVING GIFTS.

AFTER REVIEWING THIS LIST, I THINK MY PERSONAL LOVE LANGUAGE IS:

_____

_____

AND I THINK MY BOYFRIEND'S IS:

_____

_____

BASED UPON WHAT I THINK HIS LOVE LANGUAGE IS, THE THINGS I SHOULD MAKE SURE I DO MORE OFTEN ARE...

_____

_____

_____

_____

_____

I believe...

- ☐ IN SOUL MATES.
- ☐ IN LOVE AT FIRST SIGHT.
- ☐ THAT LOVE CAN LAST FOREVER.
- ☐ IT IS OKAY TO KISS ON THE FIRST DATE.
- ☐ IN LONG-DISTANCE RELATIONSHIPS.
- ☐ IN MARRIAGE.
- ☐ IN DIVORCE.
- ☐ THAT YOU CAN BE FRIENDS WITH AN EX.
- ☐ IT IS IMPORTANT TO CELEBRATE VALENTINE'S DAY.
- ☐ IN WILD ROMANTIC GESTURES.
- ☐ THAT YOU CAN FIND LOVE THROUGH ONLINE DATING.
- ☐ IT IS OKAY TO LIVE TOGETHER WITHOUT BEING MARRIED.
- ☐ IN SECOND CHANCES.
- ☐ IN THIRD CHANCES.
- ☐ THAT PEOPLE TEND TO HAVE A SPECIFIC TYPE THEY ARE ATTRACTED TO.
- ☐ MORE GUYS SHOULD LIKE ROMANTIC COMEDIES.
- ☐ THAT IT IS OKAY TO MOVE TO BE WITH SOMEONE.
- ☐ COUPLES SHOULD KNOW ABOUT EACH OTHER'S PAST RELATIONSHIPS.
- ☐ IT IS OKAY TO HAVE A RELATIONSHIP WITH SOMEONE YOU CLOSELY WORK WITH.
- ☐ TRUST CAN BE RESTORED.

I believe...

- ☐ IT IS IMPORTANT THAT A COUPLE GETS ALONG WITH EACH OTHER'S FRIENDS.
- ☐ IN THE OLD SAYING THAT WOMEN TEND TO DATE PEOPLE LIKE THEIR FATHER AND MEN PEOPLE LIKE THEIR MOTHER.
- ☐ THAT TEXTS AND CALLS SHOULD BE RESPONDED TO AS SOON AS POSSIBLE.
- ☐ IT IS IMPORTANT THAT A COUPLE CHECK IN WITH EACH OTHER ON A REGULAR BASIS.
- ☐ THAT COMPLETE HONESTY IS THE BEST POLICY.
- ☐ IN LOVE POEMS.
- ☐ IN LOVE SONGS.
- ☐ THAT A COUPLE SHOULD KNOW THE DETAILS OF EACH OTHER'S FINANCES.
- ☐ THAT IT IS OK TO HAVE SEPARATE VACATIONS.
- ☐ THAT LOVE IS BLIND.
- ☐ IT IS OKAY TO DATE SOMEONE WHO USED TO DATE A CLOSE FRIEND.
- ☐ THAT ONE OF THE MAIN POINTS TO GETTING MARRIED IS TO HAVE CHILDREN TOGETHER.
- ☐ YOUR PARTNER'S NEEDS COME FIRST.
- ☐ IT IS CRITICAL THAT BOTH PEOPLE IN A RELATIONSHIP HAVE THE SAME RELIGIOUS AND SPIRITUAL BELIEFS.
- ☐ IT IS OKAY TO NEED SOME ALONE TIME.
- ☐ THAT IT IS HEALTHY FOR INDIVIDUALS IN A RELATIONSHIP TO GROW AND CHANGE.

My boyfriend in 26 letters...

WRITE A WORD (OR MORE IF YOU WANT) THAT DESCRIBES YOUR BOYFRIEND THAT BEGINS WITH EACH LETTER:

A:

B:

C:

D:

E:

F:

G:

H:

I:

J:

K:

L:

My boyfriend in 26 letters...

M:

N:

P:

Q:

R:

S:

T:

U:

V:

W:

X:

Y:

Z:

Some stuff about me...

IF I WERE TO WRITE AN AUTOBIOGRAPHY, THE TITLE WOULD BE...

_____

_____

_____

ONE OF MY FAVORITE QUOTES IS...

_____

_____

_____

_____

MY PERSONAL HERO IS...

_____

_____

_____

AND MY PERSONAL VILLAIN IS...

_____

_____

_____

THE SMARTEST THING I HAVE EVER DONE IS...

_____

_____

_____

_____

_____

_____

AND THE DUMBEST THING IS...

_____

_____

_____

_____

_____

_____

_____

THE BRAVEST THING I HAVE EVER DONE IS...

_____
_____
_____
_____
_____
_____

ONE OF THE HARDEST DECISIONS OF MY LIFE WAS...

_____
_____
_____
_____
_____
_____
_____

THE HARDEST THING I HAVE HAD TO OVERCOME IN MY LIFE IS...

___

___

___

___

___

I SUCCEEDED IN OVERCOMING THIS CHALLENGE BECAUSE OF THESE DECISIONS, ACTIONS, AND PEOPLE...

___

___

___

___

___

___

___

___

I have...

- ☐ TRAVELED OVERSEAS.
- ☐ FLOWN IN A PLANE.
- ☐ HAD SURGERY.
- ☐ MILKED A COW.
- ☐ BEEN IN A FIST FIGHT.
- ☐ GONE ON A BLIND DATE.
- ☐ HAD MY TONSILS REMOVED.
- ☐ MADE A SPEECH IN FRONT OF A LARGE GROUP.
- ☐ SUNG A SOLO IN FRONT OF AN AUDIENCE.
- ☐ BEEN ARRESTED.
- ☐ RIDDEN A MOTORCYCLE.
- ☐ SHOT A GUN.
- ☐ RIDDEN IN A HOT AIR BALLOON.
- ☐ GONE ON A CRUISE.
- ☐ LIED TO A POLICE OFFICER.
- ☐ GONE SCUBA DIVING.
- ☐ HAD STICHES.
- ☐ RUN A MARATHON.
- ☐ AGREED TO BE SOMEONE ELSE'S ALIBI.
- ☐ GONE BUNGEE JUMPING.

I have...

- ☐ SKIPPED SCHOOL.
- ☐ LOST A SIGNIFICANT AMOUNT OF WEIGHT.
- ☐ RIDDEN IN A HELICOPTER.
- ☐ GOTTEN A TATTOO.
- ☐ BEEN TO A BROADWAY MUSICAL.
- ☐ USED A FAKE ID.
- ☐ BEEN TO A PROFESSIONAL SPORTING EVENT.
- ☐ MET A CELEBRITY.
- ☐ GONE SKYDIVING.
- ☐ BROKEN A BONE.
- ☐ CHEATED ON A TEST.
- ☐ BEEN TO A LARGE MUSIC FESTIVAL.
- ☐ SNOOPED THROUGH SOMEONE'S MEDICINE CABINET.
- ☐ GONE SURFING.
- ☐ PERFORMED IN A PLAY, MUSICAL, OR OPERA.
- ☐ LIED TO GET OUT OF WORK.
- ☐ GONE BACKPACKING.
- ☐ SNUCK INTO A MOVIE.
- ☐ BEEN TO THE GRAND CANYON.
- ☐ PARTICIPATED IN A POLITICAL PROTEST.

I have...

- ☐ STOOD UP A DATE.
- ☐ BEEN STOOD UP.
- ☐ GOTTEN A SPEEDING TICKET.
- ☐ GOTTEN OUT OF A SPEEDING TICKET.
- ☐ CRASHED A PARTY.
- ☐ HAD A CRUSH ON A CELEBRITY.
- ☐ HAD A CRUSH ON A TEACHER OR BOSS.
- ☐ BEEN SELECTED FOR A JURY.
- ☐ GIVEN SOMEONE A FAKE NAME OR PHONE NUMBER.
- ☐ BEEN IN A BAND.
- ☐ HAD A NEAR DEATH EXPERIENCE.
- ☐ PERFORMED CPR OR THE HEIMLICH MANEUVER ON SOMEONE.
- ☐ DRIVEN IN A COUNTRY WHERE THEY DRIVE ON THE OTHER SIDE OF THE ROAD.
- ☐ PLAYED SPIN THE BOTTLE.
- ☐ DRIVEN ON ROUTE 66.
- ☐ SEEN A METEOR SHOWER.
- ☐ CROWD-SURFED AT A MUSIC CONCERT.
- ☐ SLEPT OUTSIDE UNDER THE STARS.
- ☐ HAD MY APPENDIX REMOVED.

I have...

- ☐ LEARNED A SECOND LANGUAGE.
- ☐ BEEN STUCK IN AN ELEVATOR.
- ☐ HAD MY PALM READ.
- ☐ BROKEN OFF AN ENGAGEMENT.
- ☐ HAD BRACES.
- ☐ GONE ICE SKATING.
- ☐ GONE SNOW SKIING.
- ☐ GONE SLEDDING.
- ☐ BEEN TO A TROPICAL ISLAND.
- ☐ RIDDEN ON A TRAIN.
- ☐ GROWN A VEGETABLE GARDEN.
- ☐ STARTED A BUSINESS.
- ☐ EXPERIENCED AN EARTHQUAKE.
- ☐ BEEN IN A HURRICANE.
- ☐ BEEN WHERE A TORNADO STRUCK DOWN.
- ☐ DONATED BLOOD.
- ☐ MADE A SNOW ANGEL.
- ☐ LIVED IN A FOREIGN COUNTRY.
- ☐ BEEN TO A HOT SPRING.
- ☐ BEEN KNOCKED UNCONSCIOUS.

I have...

- ☐ GONE SAILING.
- ☐ BEEN TO A RODEO.
- ☐ GONE DEEP SEA FISHING.
- ☐ DRIVEN A TRACTOR.
- ☐ BEEN IN THE MIDDLE OF A MOSH PIT.
- ☐ BEEN CALLED UP ON STAGE AT A CONCERT/SHOW.
- ☐ BEEN TO A TOPLESS/NUDE BEACH.
- ☐ RIDDEN A MECHANICAL BULL.
- ☐ BEEN A PASSENGER IN A PRIVATE JET.
- ☐ DYED MY HAIR.
- ☐ HAD MY PICTURE TAKEN WITH SOMEONE FAMOUS.
- ☐ BEEN A MAID OF HONOR/BEST MAN.
- ☐ RE-GIFTED A GIFT.
- ☐ BEEN ON TELEVISION.
- ☐ SEEN A UFO.
- ☐ GONE SKINNY-DIPPING.
- ☐ ATTENDED THE BALLET.
- ☐ ADOPTED A PET.
- ☐ ATTENDED THE OPERA.
- ☐ RIDDEN IN A HORSE-DRAWN CARRIAGE.

"To the world you may be one person, but to one person you are the world." – Author Unknown

I am grateful for...

THESE EVERYDAY THINGS...

_____

_____

_____

_____

_____

THESE CHALLENGES I HAVE EXPERIENCED...

_____

_____

_____

_____

_____

_____

I am grateful for...

THIS RISK I TOOK:

_____

_____

_____

_____

THIS SACRIFICE I MADE:

_____

_____

_____

_____

THIS HARD DECISION I MADE:

_____

_____

_____

_____

I am grateful for...

THIS BIG CHANGE THAT HAPPENED IN MY LIFE:

_____
_____
_____

THIS THING ABOUT MYSELF:

_____
_____
_____
_____

THIS TALENT OR SKILL I HAVE:

_____
_____
_____
_____

I am grateful for...

THESE THINGS ABOUT MY GIRLFRIEND...

Questions about me...

THE PERSON I TELL (MOSTLY) EVERYTHING IS...

_____

_____

IF I COULD TRAVEL TO ANYPLACE IN THE WORLD WITH ALL EXPENSES PAID, I WOULD CHOOSE TO VISIT...

_____

_____

I AM A LITTLE EMBARRASSED THAT THIS SCARES THE HECK OUT OF ME...

_____

MY OPINION OF ROLLERCOASTERS IS...

_____

_____

MY GO-TO COUPLE'S KARAOKE SONG IS...

_____

_____

MY FAVORITE SEASON OF THE YEAR IS...

_____

MY FAVORITE CANDY IS...

_____

THE DISH I COOK BETTER THAN MOST IS...

_____

_____

MY FAVORITE WAY TO GET SOME EXERCISE IS...

_____

EVEN THOUGH EIGHTEEN IS WHEN YOU LEGALLY BECOME AN ADULT, THE AGE WHEN I ACTUALLY BEGAN ACTING LIKE AN ONE WAS...

_____

THE NUMBER ONE WORST PART OF BEING AN ADULT IS...

_____

_____

AND THE NUMBER ONE BEST PART IS...

_____

_____

THE LAST SOUVENIR I BOUGHT WAS...

_____

_____

MY FAVORITE HOLIDAY MOVIE IS...

_____

_____

THE CORRECT WAY TO SQUEEZE THE TOOTHPASTE FROM THE TUBE IS...

_____

THE THING I HABITUALLY DO THAT CAN ANNOY MY BOYFRIEND IS...

_____

_____

MY GO-TO OUTFIT IS...

_____

_____

_____

MY DREAM. CAREER IS...

_____

_____

THE HOUSEHOLD CHORE I DISLIKE THE MOST IS...

_____

MY FAVORITE HOLIDAY TRADITION IS...

_____

MY FAVORITE COLOR FOR MY CLOTHING IS...

_____

A SONG THAT REMINDS ME OF MY BOYFRIEND IS...

_____

_____

IF I COULD ONLY PICK ONE FAVORITE MEMORY OF A TIME I SPENT WITH MY BOYFRIEND, I WOULD PICK...

_____

_____

_____

_____

_____

_____

Questions about him (also known as, "I am pretty sure this is right") ...

THE PERSON HE TELLS (MOSTLY) EVERYTHING IS...

_____

_____

IF HE COULD TRAVEL TO ANYPLACE IN THE WORLD WITH ALL EXPENSES PAID, HE WOULD CHOOSE TO VISIT...

_____

_____

HE SHOULD BE A LITTLE EMBARRASSED THAT THIS SCARES THE HECK OUT OF HIM...

_____

HIS OPINION OF ROLLERCOASTERS IS...

_____

_____

HIS GO-TO COUPLE'S KARAOKE SONG IS...

_____

_____

HIS FAVORITE SEASON OF THE YEAR IS...

_____

HIS FAVORITE CANDY IS...

_____

THE DISH HE COOKS BETTER THAN MOST IS...

_____

_____

HIS FAVORITE WAY TO GET SOME EXERCISE IS...

_____

EVEN THOUGH EIGHTEEN IS WHEN YOU LEGALLY BECOME AN ADULT, THE AGE WHEN HE ACTUALLY BEGAN ACTING LIKE AN ONE WAS...

_____

HE THINKS THAT THIS IS THE NUMBER ONE WORST PART OF BEING AN ADULT...

_____

_____

AND THIS IS THE NUMBER ONE BEST PART IS...

_____

_____

THE LAST SOUVENIR HE BOUGHT WAS...

_____

HIS FAVORITE HOLIDAY MOVIE IS...

_____

_____

HE THINKS THAT THE CORRECT WAY TO SQUEEZE THE TOOTHPASTE FROM THE TUBE IS...

_____

THE THING HE HABITUALLY DOES THAT CAN ANNOY SOMETIMES ANNOY ME IS...

_____

_____

HIS GO-TO OUTFIT IS...

_____

_____

_____

HIS DREAM. CAREER IS...

_____

_____

THE HOUSEHOLD CHORE HE DISLIKES THE MOST IS...

_____

HIS FAVORITE HOLIDAY TRADITION IS...

_____

HIS FAVORITE COLOR FOR HIS CLOTHES IS...

_____

THE SONG THAT REMINDS HIM OF ME IS...

_____

_____

IF HE HAD TO PICK JUST ONE FAVORITE MEMORY OF A TIME I WE SPENT TOGETHER, HE WOULD CHOOSE...

_____

_____

_____

_____

_____

_____

A few of my personal proudest accomplishments are...

1. _____

2. _____

3. _____

4. _____

5. _____

6. _____

7. _____

8. _____

9. _____

10. _____

11. _____

12. _____

13. _____

14. _____

15. _____

And here are a few of things I am proud of my boyfriend for accomplishing...

1. _____
2. _____
3. _____
4. _____
5. _____
6. _____
7. _____
8. _____
9. _____
10. _____
11. _____
12. _____
13. _____
14. _____
15. _____

My travel stories...

MY LAST BIG VACATION TRIP WAS TO...,

___

MY THOUGHTS ON FLYING FOR SHORT DISTANCES ARE...

___

___

AND FOR LONG DISTANCES...

___

___

THE CURRENT STATE OF MY PASSPORT IS (ACTIVE, EXPIRED, NEED TO GET ONE) ...,

___

LATELY, I HAVE BEEN THINKING THAT IT WOULD GREAT TO TAKE A TRIP TO...

___

___

AND THE PLACE I WOULD TRAVEL TO IF TIME AND MONEY WERE NO CONCERN IS...

___

___

A FEW OF THE PLACES I HAVE TRAVELED TO ARE...

1. _____
2. _____
3. _____
4. _____
5. _____
6. _____
7. _____
8. _____
9. _____
10. _____
11. _____
12. _____
13. _____
14. _____
15. _____

More questions about me...

MY GO-TO MOVIE TO WATCH WHEN I NEED A SMILE IS...
_____

MY FAVORITE FLOWER OR PLANT IS...
_____

I MOVED THIS MANY TIMES BEFORE THE AGE OF EIGHTEEN...
_____

THE NUMBER ONE THING ON MY BUCKET LIST IS...
_____

MY BLOOD TYPE IS ...
_____

IF I HAD TO LIVE IN A TELEVISIONS SHOW, I WOULD WANT IT TO BE...
_____
_____

THE NUMBER ONE THING I WANT TO CHANGE IN MY LIFE IS...
_____
_____

More questions about him (How do you think he would answer?)...

HIS GO-TO MOVIE TO WATCH WHEN HE NEEDS A SMILE IS...

___

HIS FAVORITE FLOWER OR PLANT IS...

___

HE MOVED THIS MANY TIMES BEFORE THE AGE OF EIGHTEEN...

___

THE NUMBER ONE THING ON HIS BUCKET LIST IS...

___

HIS BLOOD TYPE IS ...

___

IF HE HAD TO LIVE IN THE WORLD OF ONE TELEVISIONS SHOW, HE WOULD WANT IT TO BE...

___

___

THE NUMBER ONE THING HE WANTS TO CHANGE IN HIS LIFE IS...

___

___

More questions about me...

THE THING I THINK I SPEND TOO MUCH MONEY ON IS...
_____

IF I COULD USE ONLY ONE HEALTH AND BEAUTY PRODUCT FOR THE NEXT YEAR, IT WOULD BE...
_____
_____

THE RELATIONSHIP I NEED TO WORK ON IS WITH...
_____

IF I COULD CHOOSE TO REMAIN ONE AGE FOR THE REST OF MY LIFE, IT WOULD BE...
_____

MY MOST PRIZED POSSESSION IS...
_____

MY GUILTY PLEASURE READING IS...
_____
_____

THE EVENT I WANT TO GO BACK IN TIME TO WITNESS IS...
_____

More questions about him (How do you think he would answer?)...

THE THING HE THINKS HE SPENDS TOO MUCH MONEY ON IS...

IF HE COULD USE ONLY ONE HEALTH AND BEAUTY PRODUCT FOR THE NEXT YEAR, IT WOULD BE...

THE RELATIONSHIP HE THINKS HE NEEDS TO WORK ON IS WITH...

IF HE COULD CHOOSE TO REMAIN ONE AGE FOR THE REST OF HIS LIFE, IT WOULD BE...

HIS MOST PRIZED POSSESSION IS...

HIS GUILTY PLEASURE READING IS...

THE EVENT HE WOULD GO BACK IN TIME TO WITNESS IS...

My top 5 foods I want to try or restaurants I want to eat at are...

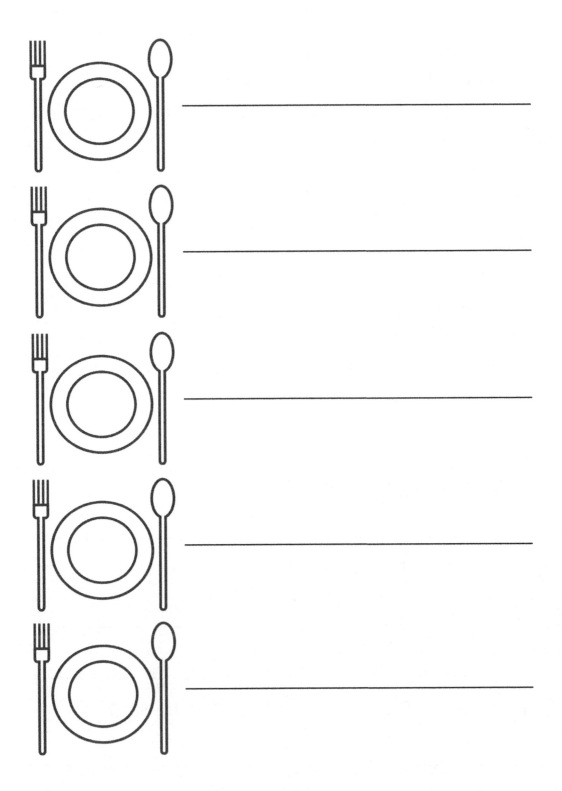

The top 5 foods he wants to try or restaurants he wants to eat at are......

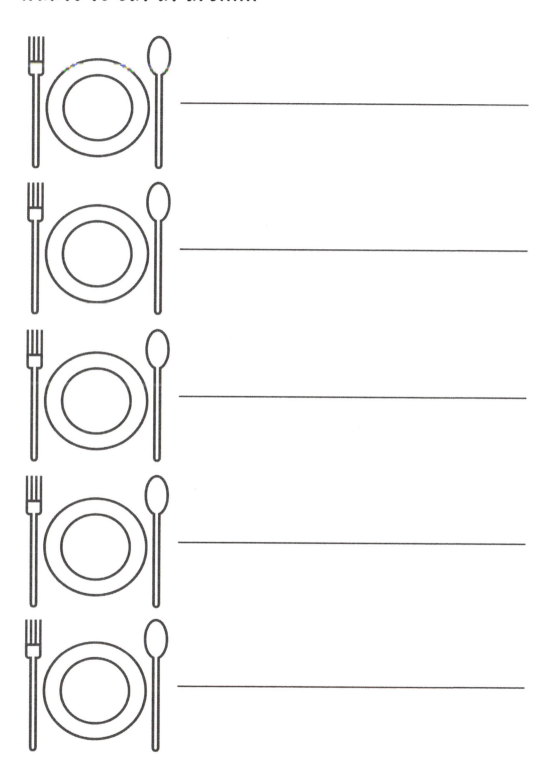

Top 10

THE TEN BOOKS THAT HAVE I LOVE AND/OR MAJORLY IMPACTED THE WAY I THINK, WORK, OR LIVE MY LIFE ARE...

1. _____

2. _____

3. _____

4. _____

5. _____

6. _____

7. _____

8. _____

9. _____

10. _____

IF I HAD TO PICK TEN OF MY FAVORITE TELEVISION SHOWS OF ALL TIME, I WOULD PICK...

1. _____

2. _____

3. _____

4. _____

5. _____

6. _____

7. _____

8. _____

9. _____

10. _____

IF I HAD TO PICK TEN OF MY FAVORITE MOVIES OF ALL TIME, I WOULD PICK...

1. _____

2. _____

3. _____

4. _____

5. _____

6. _____

7. _____

8. _____

9. _____

10. _____

IF I HAD TO PICK TEN OF MY FAVORITE BANDS OR MUSICIANS OF ALL TIME, I WOULD PICK...

1. _____

2. _____

3. _____

4. _____

5. _____

6. _____

7. _____

8. _____

9. _____

10. _____

IF I HAD TO PICK TEN OF MY FAVORITE VIDEO GAMES OF ALL TIME, I WOULD PICK...

1. _____

2. _____

3. _____

4. _____

5. _____

6. _____

7. _____

8. _____

9. _____

10. _____

IF I HAD TO PICK TEN OF MY FAVORITE TIMES SPENT WITH MY BOYFRIEND, I WOULD PICK...

1. _____

2. _____

3. _____

4. _____

5. _____

6. _____

7. _____

8. _____

9. _____

10. _____

Fifteen things I want...

TO DO THIS YEAR...

1. _____

2. _____

3. _____

4. _____

5. _____

6. _____

7. _____

8. _____

9. _____

10. _____

11. _____

12. _____

13. _____

14. _____

15. _____

TO DO OVER THE NEXT TEN YEARS...

1. _____

2. _____

3. _____

4. _____

5. _____

6. _____

7. _____

8. _____

9. _____

10. _____

11. _____

12. _____

13. _____

14. _____

15. _____

SKILLS OR ABILITIES I WANT TO LEARN...

1. _____
2. _____
3. _____
4. _____
5. _____
6. _____
7. _____
8. _____
9. _____
10. _____
11. _____
12. _____
13. _____
14. _____
15. _____

TO TRAVEL TO...

1. _____
2. _____
3. _____
4. _____
5. _____
6. _____
7. _____
8. _____
9. _____
10. _____
11. _____
12. _____
13. _____
14. _____
15. _____

TO EXPERIENCE...

1. _____
2. _____
3. _____
4. _____
5. _____
6. _____
7. _____
8. _____
9. _____
10. _____
11. _____
12. _____
13. _____
14. _____
15. _____

TO ATTEND OR SEE...

1. _____
2. _____
3. _____
4. _____
5. _____
6. _____
7. _____
8. _____
9. _____
10. _____
11. _____
12. _____
13. _____
14. _____
15. _____

OTHER THINGS I ABSOLUTELY NEED TO DO, SEE, LEARN, VISIT, ETC...

1. _____
2. _____
3. _____
4. _____
5. _____
6. _____
7. _____
8. _____
9. _____
10. _____
11. _____
12. _____
13. _____
14. _____
15. _____

16. _____
17. _____
18. _____
19. _____
20. _____
21. _____
22. _____
23. _____
24. _____
25. _____
26. _____
27. _____
28. _____
29. _____
30. _____

Looking forward...

THIS IS WHAT I WANT MY LIFE TO LOOK FIVE YEARS FROM TODAY...

_____

_____

_____

_____

_____

_____

_____

_____

_____

_____

_____

THIS IS WHAT I WANT MY LIFE TO LOOK TWENTY-FIVE YEARS FROM TODAY...

This is the Ta Dah Page

YEP, YOU'RE DONE.

YOU'VE ANSWERED EVERY QUESTION, COMPLETED ALL THE ACTIVITIES (AT LEAST MOST OF THEM), AND YOU'VE SHARED YOUR MEMORIES AND YOUR THOUGHTS.

YOU'VE HAD SOME FUN AND ALLOWED YOURSELF TO OPEN UP AND TALK ABOUT YOURSELF.

MOST OF ALL, YOU NOW KNOW HOW GREAT IT FEELS WHEN ANOTHER PERSON SAYS, "I WANT TO LEARN MORE ABOUT YOU."

(AND HOW THAT IS ESPECIALLY GREAT WHEN IT IS SOMEONE YOU CARE ABOUT.)

WHAT ARE THE NEXT STEPS?

THE FIRST IS TO SHARE YOUR HANDIWORK WITH THE PERSON WHO GAVE YOU THIS BOOK. LOOK THROUGH IT TOGETHER AND TALK ABOUT YOUR RESPONSES.

ADD MORE DETAILS AND DO SOME STORYTELLING WITH YOUR USUAL FLAIR.

ANOTHER IDEA IS TO GET HIM A COPY OF "TO MY BOYFRIEND, I WANT TO HEAR YOUR LIFE STORY." HE WILL BE THRILLED AND HUMBLED THAT YOU WANT TO KNOW MORE ABOUT HIM AND HIS LIFE.

NO GO REWARD YOURSELF AND DO SOMETHING FUN WITH YOUR BOYFRIEND. WHO KNOWS WHAT MEMORIES AND MOMENTS YOU WILL COLLECT IN THE PROCESS.

"You and I, it's as though we have been taught to kiss in heaven and sent down to earth together, to see if we know what we were taught." - "Doctor Zhivago" by Boris Pasternak

Hear Your Story Books

AT **HEAR YOUR STORY**®, WE HAVE CREATED A LINE OF BOOKS FOCUSED ON GIVING EACH OF US A PLACE TO TELL THE UNIQUE STORY OF WHO WE ARE, WHERE WE HAVE BEEN, AND WHERE WE ARE GOING.

SHARING AND HEARING THE STORIES OF THE PEOPLE IN OUR LIFE CREATES CLOSENESS AND UNDERSTANDING, ULTIMATELY STRENGTHENING OUR BONDS.

Available at Amazon, all bookstores, and at HearYourStoryBooks.com

- TO MY BOYFRIEND, I WANT TO HEAR YOUR STORY
- MOM, I WANT TO HEAR YOUR STORY: A MOTHER'S GUIDED JOURNAL TO SHARE HER LIFE & HER LOVE
- DAD, I WANT TO HEAR YOUR STORY: A FATHER'S GUIDED JOURNAL TO SHARE HIS LIFE & HIS LOVE
- GRANDMOTHER, I WANT TO HEAR YOUR STORY: A GRANDMOTHER'S GUIDED JOURNAL TO SHARE HER LIFE AND HER LOVE
- GRANDFATHER, I WANT TO HEAR YOUR STORY: A GRANDFATHER'S GUIDED JOURNAL TO SHARE HIS LIFE AND HIS LOVE
- LIFE GAVE ME YOU; I WANT TO HEAR YOUR STORY: A GUIDED JOURNAL FOR STEPMOTHERS TO SHARE THEIR LIFE STORY
- YOU CHOOSE TO BE MY DAD; I WANT TO HEAR YOUR STORY: A GUIDED JOURNAL FOR STEPDADS TO SHARE THEIR LIFE STORY

Hear Your Story Books

- TELL YOUR LIFE STORY: THE WRITE YOUR OWN AUTOBIOGRAPHY GUIDED JOURNAL

- MOM, I WANT TO LEARN YOUR RECIPES: A KEEPSAKE MEMORY BOOK TO GATHER AND PRESERVE YOUR FAVORITE FAMILY RECIPES

- DAD, I WANT TO LEARN YOUR RECIPES: A KEEPSAKE MEMORY BOOK TO GATHER AND PRESERVE YOUR FAVORITE FAMILY RECIPES

- GRANDMOTHER, I WANT TO LEARN YOUR RECIPES: A KEEPSAKE MEMORY BOOK TO GATHER AND PRESERVE YOUR FAVORITE FAMILY RECIPES

- GRANDFATHER, I WANT TO LEARN YOUR RECIPES: A KEEPSAKE MEMORY BOOK TO GATHER AND PRESERVE YOUR FAVORITE FAMILY RECIPES

- AUNT, I WANT TO LEARN YOUR RECIPES: A KEEPSAKE MEMORY BOOK TO GATHER AND PRESERVE YOUR FAVORITE FAMILY RECIPES

- UNCLE, I WANT TO LEARN YOUR RECIPES: A KEEPSAKE MEMORY BOOK TO GATHER AND PRESERVE YOUR FAVORITE FAMILY RECIPES

- TELL YOUR LIFE STORY: THE WRITE YOUR OWN AUTOBIOGRAPHY GUIDED JOURNAL

- TO MY WONDERFUL AUNT, I WANT TO HEAR YOUR STORY: A GUIDED JOURNAL TO SHARE HER LIFE AND HER LOVE

- TO MY UNCLE, I WANT TO HEAR YOUR STORY: A GUIDED JOURNAL TO SHARE HIS LIFE AND HIS LOVE

- THE STORY OF EXPECTING YOU: A SELFCARE PREGNANCY GUIDED JOURNAL AND MEMORY BOOK

About the Author

JEFFREY MASON IS THE CREATOR AND AUTHOR OF THE BEST-SELLING HEAR YOUR STORY® LINE OF BOOKS AND IS THE FOUNDER OF THE COMPANY HEAR YOUR STORY®.

IN RESPONSE TO HIS OWN FATHER'S FIGHT WITH ALZHEIMER'S, JEFFREY WROTE HIS FIRST TWO BOOKS, MOM, I WANT TO HEAR YOUR STORY AND DAD, I WANT TO HEAR YOUR STORY IN 2019. SINCE THEN, HE HAS WRITTEN AND DESIGNED OVER 30 BOOKS, BEEN PUBLISHED IN FOUR LANGUAGES, AND SOLD OVER 300,000 COPIES WORLDWIDE.

JEFFREY IS DEDICATED TO SPREADING THE MISSION THAT THE LITTLE THINGS ARE THE BIG THINGS AND THAT EACH OF US HAS AN INCREDIBLE LIFE STORY THAT NEEDS TO BE SHARED AND CELEBRATED. HE CONTINUES TO CREATE BOOKS THAT HE HOPES WILL GUIDE PEOPLE TO REFLECT ON AND SHARE THEIR FULL LIFE EXPERIENCE, WHILE CREATING OPPORTUNITIES FOR TALKING, LISTENING, LEARNING, AND UNDERSTANDING.

HEAR YOUR STORY® CAN BE VISITED AT HEARYOURSTORYBOOKS.COM AND JEFFREY CAN BE CONTACTED FOR QUESTIONS, COMMENTS, PODCASTING, SPEAKING ENGAGEMENTS, OR JUST A HELLO AT JEFFREY.MASON@HEARYOURSTORY.COM.

HE WOULD BE GRATEFUL IF YOU WOULD HELP PEOPLE FIND HIS BOOKS BY LEAVING A REVIEW ON AMAZON. YOUR FEEDBACK HELPS HIM GET BETTER AT THIS THING HE LOVES.

COPYRIGHT © 2022 EYP PUBLISHING, LLC, HEAR YOUR STORY BOOKS, & JEFFREY MASON. ALL RIGHTS RESERVED. NO PART OF THIS PUBLICATION MAY BE REPRODUCED, DISTRIBUTED, OR TRANSMITTED IN ANY FORM OR BY ANY MEANS, INCLUDING PHOTOCOPYING, RECORDING, COMPUTER, OR OTHER ELECTRONIC OR MECHANICAL METHODS, WITHOUT THE PRIOR WRITTEN PERMISSION OF THE PUBLISHER, EXCEPT IN THE CASE OF BRIEF QUOTATIONS EMBODIED IN CRITICAL REVIEWS AND CERTAIN OTHER NONCOMMERCIAL USES PERMITTED BY COPYRIGHT LAW. FOR PERMISSION REQUESTS, WRITE TO THE PUBLISHER, ADDRESSED "ATTENTION: PERMISSIONS COORDINATOR," TO CUSTOMERSERVICE@EYPPUBLISHING.COM.

ISBN: 978-1-955034-47-0

Made in the USA
Middletown, DE
30 May 2024

55072430R00073